Written by: **KELLY ARMBRUSTER**

illustrated by: **RAMAN BHARDWAJ**

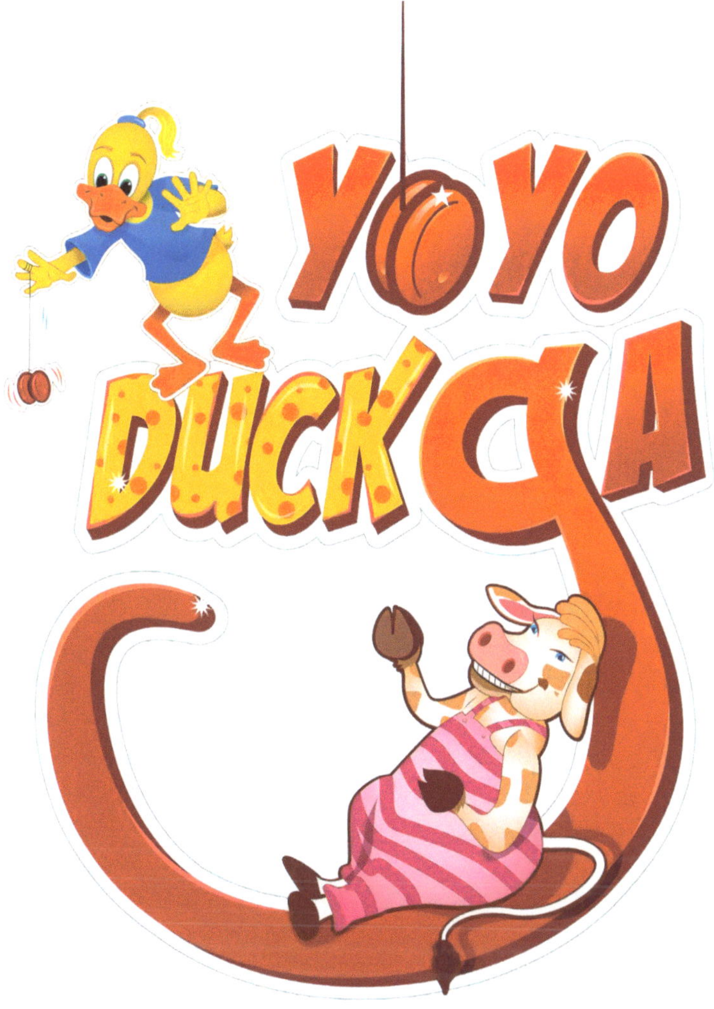

GetArmbruster.com

Published by BooxAI
ISBN: 978-965-578-216-5

<u>PREFACE</u>

Ready to **quiet the quack**™ and dive into the world of Dancer the Duck?

Yoduckga™ was created to include a mascot as a beacon for kindness, mindfulness, meditation and inclusion. Dancer is a fun loving duck who has friends that are other animals that align with yoga poses. Dancer and friends go on adventures and share lessons that will help your child deal with their emotions, and also teach valuable lessons in overcoming fear and conquering challenges. Currently Dancer the Duck has produced three rap songs that can be downloaded at www.yoduckga.com.

As the first of a series of three books, Yo-YoDuckGa takes your child on an unforgettable journey that has Dancer the Duck want to take on a new challenge. This book is also about friendship and Dancer the Duck has a great friend in Jill-O the cow. From managing frustrations to accomplishing goals, Yo-YoDuckGa has everything for your child to remember to persevere and succeed with uplifting tips for breathing through stressful situations.

About my dedication to Dancer the Duck and his friends:
We are building a movement that encourages kindness while embracing diversity and promoting inclusion. My affectionate term for this journey is called my #duckhustle, and don't be surprised if you see Dancer the Duck reach his lifetime goals of attending the Special Olympics or starring in an animated short film.

If your child is a fan of the *Yo Gabba Gabba* series, Yo-YoDuckGa is sure to become their uplifting and fun guide for years to come. Whether you are the parent of a kindergartener, first grader, or a child with special needs you're sure to find something that will surprise you and your little one time after time!

What's my personal motivation, you ask?

Inspiration for Yoduckga™ came from a particularly captivating chapter in my life when I learned that if I changed the fear-based chatter in my head, I could accomplish more. The fear-based thoughts or "quacks" can be quieted with breathing and through Yoga and Meditation. Mindfulness of "Quieting the Quack" can also reshape an entire generation of children if they learn self-awareness at an early age and use that awareness to tap into their ultimate potential.

Help your child quiet the quack™ today!

-Kelly Armbruster

This is a story
about Dancer the Duck
who tried playing with a yo-yo,
but didn't have much luck.

Dancer was frustrated,
his patience worn thin.
He thought, "I can't do this.
I can't make this yo-yo spin."

He sighed, and he stomped,
his nervousness showed.
The yo-yo got tangled
with every new throw.

After an hour of trying
to master "The Spin"
Dancer turned to the Cow,
Jill-O, his best friend.

Dancer asked Jill-O,
"What can I do?
I keep trying and trying,
but can't master the moves."

The Elevator, Walk the Dog,
Eiffel Tower or Rock the Baby,
the challenge to do one trick,
it's driving me crazy!

Jill-O smiled, then laughed,
she was very amused.
Just think, you have fingers,
I do it with hooves.

Dancer stood there a moment
and let it sink in.
Jill-O was right,
so he tried it again.

Jill-O added,
"When you're mad, angry,
frustrated or scared,
there are thoughts in your head
that shouldn't be there.

Just stop what you are doing
and find a mat or a towel,
then breathe these 5 letters,
let's start with the vowels!"

A E I O U

A is for AWESOME *and that is what you are. Taking this first breath makes you a star.*

E is for EXERCISE *which helps you adjust. When you're feeling anxious, breathing a must.*

I is for INSPIRED *and means that you are excited. By music or math - only good thoughts invited.*

O is for OPEN-MINDED *it's like opening a new door. Don't judge the experience of doors you've opened before.*

U is for UNAFRAID *to try new things; no reason to be scared. Word to the wise: keep marshmallows out of your hair.*

Dancer gave Jill-O a hug
feeling calm and in control,
"Thank you Jill-O,
I have a new goal!

I will share this technique
with all kids who will listen,
through yoga and music
I can make their smiles glisten!"

So, when you feel angry
when you feel sad
when things don't go right
or things just feel bad.

Remember your vowels,
and breathe in the wind
and if you forget,
turn to your best friend.

With a wink to his bestie
and before parting ways,
Dancer grabbed the yo-yo
and began to amaze.

With a flick of his wrist
and a calm, cool head
the yo-yo, once wobbly
now danced on the thread!

Jill-O's eyes lit up
and Dancer's did too.
Dancer quacked with elation
and Jill-O let out a MOOOOOOOOOO!

Today Dancer learned.
He was able all along,
but his overwhelming frustration
caused the tricks to go wrong.

So, remember your vowels:
Breathe out….breathe in.
And before you know it,
your own yo-yo will spin.

Use the next few pages
and color your favorite character!